Visual Poetics

Immersive Experience

Scott LeVeque

Giant Publishing Company
Lincoln, Nebraska, USA

Published by Giant Publishing Company
Post Office Box 6455
Lincoln, NE 68506
www.giantpublishingcompany.com

Printed in the United States of America

Cover art by Allyson LeVeque

ISBN: 979-8-9898098-7-5

I would like to formally acknowledge that although I utilized AI to assist with the refinement of grammar and structure, the original content, concepts, and creative expressions within these poems are solely my own. This work reflects my personal voice and artistic vision. – Author, Scott LeVeque

Acknowledgment

This book is a promise to my younger self. I want to thank my sister, Allyson, for creating the cover for this book. While my sister was painting, an imperfection appeared on the top right. However, instead of calling this piece a mistake, she painted over its flaws to make it even more valuable. This piece was one of the main reasons why I chose the cover for this book. With Allyson included, I also want to thank my father Dan, my mother Kathy, and my step-dad Curt, for making this possible. Although this book could have been published years earlier, my family never gave up on the idea that all things are possible.

Introduction

For a long time, I wasn't sure why I wanted to publish a book of poetry. Poetry felt like a fading art, but an inner voice kept asking: Why haven't you made the book yet?

Seventeen years passed while I chased the idea, unsure of the process—what font to use, how large the pages should be. Those questions kept me from starting, pushing book-making to the back of my mind as I moved through daily life.

Now, after seventeen years, I've found a reason to proceed: to craft visual poetics. I've learned that others feel the same emotions, though life may look different for each of us. In the past, I shared my words with a few readers, and their hearts were touched; today, I've shared them with more, and they've felt the words on the page in a new way.

My aim is simple: to make the words on paper come alive in the reader's mind—like a movie playing in their inner cinema. That aim paused the project for what felt like an agonizing period. What I once felt as urgent turned into a dusty journal waiting for the right moment to open again. The obstacle became clearer when I began editing my poetry with an AI-assistant. Through experimentation—finding the right words to unlock the senses and immerse you—the poetics came alive in ways I hadn't imagined. I want to clarify that I only used AI assistance for creative wording and grammar; these poems are personally written by me and carry my own creative fingerprint in everything that I write.

I'm someone who thinks best when my ideas are on paper, like puzzle pieces that fall into place. Yet when the page is finished, my head tells me something is missing—the puzzle isn't complete. It isn't the poetry itself, but how it lands in others: will you grasp what I'm trying to portray? My poetry can feel jumbled—up, down, left, right—never neatly ordered, because I want the words to invite immersion rather than present a tidy map.

I don't want poetry solo; I want a story you can envision, a scene you can feel unfold. Each person will interpret the poems in this book differently, yet I hope the words illuminate a path you can follow. That was the hard part: using poetry to connect with the inner stories of others.

So, I opened the dusty journal and began this book. With a bit of help from computational tools, I found a way to project my intentions into my poetry as a story, through careful tinkering and experimentation. At last, I have found a method to share my poetics with the world.

Back to the main aim: to help people with their emotions and remind them that they are not alone. Our circumstances differ, and I'm not claiming to know what you're going through—that's fine—but my aim is to comfort when the world grows gloomy. Each poem invites reflection on the page, and your engagement matters: through your reading, you may discover who you are, uncover something you've kept hidden, and see what lies beneath your own subconscious.

I want this book to help the inner person—the you who longs to emerge. We are all human, with our problems and our successes. If you're reading this, perhaps there is something you want to release, a path toward becoming your best self, or a route to healing.

Though the book may be brief, it is a powerful reminder that we are not alone and should not be ignored. It blends therapy with poetry by design. This book was made for you. I may not reach everyone, but I hope it reaches you and offers hope.

I didn't follow a single rigid notion of what poetry should be. There was a time when I carried a pen and notebook everywhere, driven by ideas that turned into verse. Over time, those poems reflected what I was feeling in the moment. You'll see I still have a substantial body of poetry to touch the emotions of others.

You don't need to know how poetry works to feel its emotion; it's about fluidity and meaning behind the words. Anyone can write poetry: bring your experiences, choose words carefully, attend to rhythm, craft a crisp ending, and you could write a book—or keep the impulse to yourself. With this book, my hope is to support you on your journey to recover past wounds and lift your spirits. If you meet someone who needs hope, share what helped you and what sparked you to take the first step toward healing. Perhaps it's the book you're reading now. Attend a poetry gathering, speak the lines that opened your eyes, and notice the reactions around you. Although this book aims to help, your words can heal others as well.

Note: at the end of this book, you will find crisis support resources. If you or someone you know is experiencing self-harm or distress, these resources can be found there. Some wounds require help beyond the book, and I'm glad to help you find appropriate support.

With all this in mind, you'll also find blank, lined sections at the end of every poem. I want you to be a part of the book—write your own story as I did mine. These pages can be used to write, draw, or simply to immerse yourself in this emotional veil.

I hope you enjoy the scope of this book and that it touches the hearts of all who read it. Enjoy!

Immerse Yourself in The Pages

Put your own creativity into this book and make it your own. The ways you can engage with the pages are limitless.

1. Draw to your heart's content.
2. Write in this like your personal journal.
3. Write poetry and get lost in the words.
4. Do what is called out.

An important note: don't limit yourself. If you work hard enough, you can make this a reality. All great journeys start from the ground and rise toward the universe.

Another goal of this book is to help you discover your hidden meaning, and to let the pain you've felt melt away as you step into the present. Eventually, you will outgrow the scope of this book and be on your way to bigger and better things. I hope you keep this book close to your heart as a reflection of who you are. No one can ruin your day unless you let them. When times are tough, and you feel you have no control, remember that life has bumps—and even I get agitated from time to time, because I am not perfect. All the poems I have written come from the heart and carry the lessons I wanted to share. At times, I needed to get the words out of my head until my mind grew quiet; now I understand that others feel the same emotions I've felt, and I want my words to connect with you, even though we all experience different life scenes. Either way, I hope you find this book helpful and take full advantage of what it offers.

Thank you for taking the time to read this book. I bless you with a great life, and if life hits you hard, getting back up is the strongest thing you can do.

"Sometimes the best advice is looking into a mirror." Scott LeVeque

Contents

Control

Easy to attain,

difficult to keep,

Growing cold,

Searching in the vast winter,

answers may be ahead,

But questions proceed,

Numb and lost in the unknown obstacles one may want to control,

Fallen in a patch of ice, unknown under your feet,

Inside the ocean engulfing your subconscious,

fearing the unknown but wishing for control,

dark as it may seem,

You're only at the surface of it all,

No matter where the path you gaze upon may lead,

You'll find out deep within yourself,

That it doesn't exist in wanting control,

as venturing into the vast ocean could leave
you stranded with one question at hand,

Why control the obstacle?

If simply accepting change was the answer?

How do you feel?
____
____
____
____
____
____
____
____
____
____
____
____
____
____
____
____
____
____
____

Lost Hope

As you wander through the twisting labyrinth,

You feel the weight of confusion and uncertainty pressing down upon you,

The walls are high and unyielding,

stretching up into the darkness above,

You look up and see a pair of eyes gazing down upon you,

their light reflecting back at you in the gloom,

They are the only source of illumination in this place.

The ground beneath your feet is featureless,

with no clear path or guiding line to lead you through the maze,

You must rely on your instincts and intuition to find your way out,

But with every step you take,

The eyes above watch and wait,

Their cold, unblinking gaze serves as a constant reminder of the stakes at play,

You know that if you falter or lose your way,

You will be lost forever in this endless maze of life,

Only by finding hope within your heart and summoning the strength to persevere can you

Hope to find your way out of the darkness and into the light.

How do you feel?

____

____

____

____

____

____

____

____

____

____

____

____

____

____

____

____

____

Cleansing Rain

Never-ending water falls gracefully onto the ground beneath,

as if the clouds above have opened up to cleanse the earth,

The sky is a canvas of gray and white,

neither dark nor light envelops the sky,

as if the heavens themselves are mourning with the rain,

Every drop that falls is a reflection of water created by the eyes,

Each one is a reminder of the emotional stressors of life.

But amidst the sadness,

There is a sense of uplifting hope that this water brings.

Not one spoke,

The world is quiet,

as if paused in a moment of reflection,

a never-ending dream of mine present this day,

Every emotion turns into enlightenment,

Every drop of rain relentlessly cleanses the void within.

In this moment,

filled with a sense of awe,

for I have never seen anything quite like this before,

And yet,

as I stand here in the rain,

I can't help but hope that it will come again,

washing away troubles and sorrows.

How do you feel?

____

____

____

____

____

____

____

____

Blindly Seek

As I glanced upon the eyes of another,

shades of grace and blinded possibilities
enveloped my expectations,

the grasp on the trust of blinded faith,

the vocal rhythm of your voice,

enough to persuade my most profound
insecurity to unravel,

My self-beating heart chains to the other,

as my mind depicts deceit...

I see blinded love,

I feel bewildered and frustrated,

I know the truth,

but wish not to speak,

I find lies as I bury them deep in the ground
beneath...

seeking love and becoming short on endless
promises of forever,

as a hollow shell wishes to become whole
again,

as does the desire of another's heart...

seeking the facet of love,

to feel the embrace of comfort and security,

When I gaze upon you,

I will love you forever...

my only,

If you are my only...

How do you feel?

____

____

____

____

____

____

____

____

____

____

____

____

____

Universal Sorrow

Looking up at the night sky,

on a cold winter,

Gazing up at the vast expanse,

crisp and bitter,

I am awestruck by the sight of every sparkling star,

As I exhale,

my breath mingles with the frosty air,

creating a misty cloud that surrounds me,

I feel my body sink into the earth beneath me,

as if it's drawing me closer to the memories that haunt me.

I try to take in the world around me,

But all I can see are memories that seem to surround me in

every direction,

like ghosts from my past.

How do you feel?

Hidden Heart

As you read these words,

You may feel the weight of your mistakes and the burden of your heart's rubble,

But know that you are not alone,

The little things that weigh us down can be overwhelming,

But there is a way through the darkness,

focusing on good perspectives of why you are here,

no matter how small the thought may be,

We create crutches to help us through the day.

However,

Be careful not to rely on these crutches too heavily,

for they can become a burden on themselves.

If your heart pleads for light again,

know that it is not too late,

You are not permanently closed off,

and not alone in your struggles,

You can find solace in helping others,

even as you heal your pain.

Take heart and know you are strong enough
to overcome darkness,

There is always light at the end of the storm.

How do you feel?

____

____

____

____

____

____

____

____

____

____

____

____

____

____

____

____

You

Entering a maze covered in mirrors,

within are the insecurities of mortality,

The maze is constantly changing,

entering the maze was not as it once was,

Once you enter the labyrinth,

One cannot simply exit,

everywhere you move about,

The mirror reflects itself upon you,

What are the mirrors telling you?

attempting to turn away from the mirror's insight and truth,

The trail once walked in the maze is no longer apparent,

The mirrors within this vast maze have blocked themselves upon you,

As you gaze upon the mirrors around you,

glancing upon the infinite replicas of your being staring back,

a question should come to mind while
surrounded by mirrors,

Why am I looking at myself?

Announcing the question changes the image
in the maze of mirrors,

from yourself,

to a dark figure unknown to the blinded
eye...

As you are blinded by what is within the
mirror,

The maze starts to speak:

"Since you hide who you are,

closed-minded,

I cannot force any questions,

nevertheless,

the answer..."

The image disappears from the mirror,

at this moment,

to where you once stood,

glancing back at the mirrors,

all you see is the maze and the reflections of glass,

The reflection of yourself,

The shadow no longer appears relevant to the labyrinth,

How can they see,

If you cannot see yourself?

How do you feel?

____

____

____

____

____

____

____

____

____

____

____

____

____

____

____

____

In Life

In life, obstacles are challenging to overcome,

times when the only person to depend on is yourself,

rejection can be a powerful force in the world,

leaving you voided and alone.

But amidst all the pain and chaos,

There becomes a bliss of emotion,

serenity and warmth,

a feeling surrounding you like a blanket,

and making the struggles of life seem at ease.

It's love,

a feeling that can't be sheltered,

A force that can't shatter even the hardest hearts,

It's the hand that holds yours through the storm,

And the light that guides you when you are lost in the dark.

Whether you have someone by your side or not,

Love is a feeling that can never be bought.

How do you feel?

____

____

____

____

____

____

____

____

____

____

____

____

____

____

____

____

____

____

____

Growing Love

Delicate roses that wither away,

Love endures and thrives every day,

Like a serpentine vine that twists and climbs,

Yearning for that one fleeting moment in time.

Once dreaming of the person passing you by,

A smile,

a wave,

a fleeting eye,

the unfathomable fear gripping you,

You hesitate on what is not present,

Afraid that if you do not move,

The chance to be seen may come to pass.

Don't lurk in the shadows and pretend their nonexistence,

Don't hide what you feel,

or pretend not to care,

When the chance is lost,

And time has flown,

Regret turns into past flaws,

thus,

The capability of attempts is lost forever.

Take that chance,

make that move,

Seize the day before they're gone,

That you were brave enough to take a chance,

To catch them before they fade into the arms of someone else, leaving behind the chances you never took,

Wishing you had never been so blind.

How do you feel?

____

____

____

____

____

____

____

____

____

Touch

You're a mystery,

words falter at your edge– collapsing into
depths I never knew,

this jolt you've given me,

unnaturally light,

as if gravity forgot to hold me.

The shock travels from your lips to mine; my
heart leaps, loud and bright– a drum I never
heard beating in the dark.

Your arms slip around me,

hands tracing my skin,

delicate as rain; with every touch I tingle,

I never want this night to end.

Your true self, your breath, your warmth–
somehow you set me free.

Under the moon, we drift toward your glow,

impossible to resist.

How do you feel?

Colorful Moments

An autumn sun, a lantern of gold and ember,
stains the horizon with a hush of flame.
Leaves unfurl like tiny banners, copper and
scarlet, then drift, feather-light, in a slow,
sunlit spiral toward the soft, waiting grass.

Piles of leaves rise, a living quilt, crackling
beneath our weight as we descend into
bronze-smelling earth and crisp air. Every
breath tastes of roasted chestnut and rain-
warmed bark; every exhale sends a whisper
of color spiraling up.

We lie on a carpet of maple and glory,
bisque-bronze leaves stitching shadows across
our skin, as the flock of birds traces a pale,
arcing thread across the sky, moving from
limb to branch to wind.

The air carries the sigh of gusts, then settles;
leaves whirl, an anthem of amber, ochre,
jade, settling like confetti around us, a soft
rain of texture and scent and memory.

Why not leave, and simply become a part of
this living painting—breathing in the moment,

letting the day lay its quiet palm upon us,
until the autumn finally folds its colors away?

How do you feel?

Manipulate

Falling for the hearts of others, while my own
wings bruise from the fall. I wrenched out
my love, a brittle seed, so they could tread it
underfoot and call it grace.

Walls tighten like a closing tide; I am
shuttered inside a glassy room, where the
only windowsill is this stubborn ache that
keeps its candle burning.

Then they reappear, a rumor of warmth; they
step onto the brittle pavement of my heart,
grind the glass to glitter, and offer a hand that
feels almost merciful—until I rise, and the
floor yawns again.

Knees skewer on splinters of longing, a
chorus of ache in the hollow of the bones.
But one thread of hope clings: they let go,
and I spiral into the same old gravity.

Consumed by love, by their gravity, I stitch
the wreckage with trembling fingers, patch by
patch, seeking a sunrise that doesn't come
with a price tag.

I am learning the rhythm of resilience:
inhale the shards, exhale the fear, stand, even
if my shadow falters.

How do you feel?

Chasm

As the sun cripples your being,

breaking your thoughts like brittle glass in heat.

Your heart,

a tapestry of missing pieces,

where you thought you knew the map of things,

turns out to vanish into oblivion,

shattering the inner confines of your subconscious,

as if a doorway yawns to the void.

How do you feel?
____

____

____

____

____

____

____

____

Deceit

Lost in a field of deception,

cornered by what merely aims,

Though sheer trust was once breathtaking,

It is ripped away, dragged from the light.

Vast feelings surge, then spill and subside,

the heaviness settling over the exhausted heart,

a gravity that will, in time, release its hold.

Within this promising field, deceit tramples the land,

tangled barbed wires of doubt snag at my sleeves,

where trust burned bright and vanished cruelly,

like ash scattering through a doorway blown ajar.

Emotions rush like a raging river,

carving furrows in the mind, then spill to the shores

where my thoughts were braided with sunlight,

My heart is heavy, worn, and tired,

fighting to postpone the pain and turmoil it's forced to bear.

But as I stand here, battered and bruised,

this too shall pass,

wounds of my heart will heal as the clock ticks,

And I'll find my way out of this darkness at last.

How do you feel?

____

____

____

____

____

____

____

____

____

____

____

Blessed Curse

Life is a curse and a blessing, a hinge on which joy and ache align. You will be hurt, and still, there will be hands reaching out– the soft tremor of a friend's touch, the quiet gravity of a lover's gaze, the stubborn warmth of strangers who show up when you least expect it.

Along with the love of others around you for support on your journey, you will learn to walk through shadow and dawn as if stepping into a doorway you never knew existed– the corridor of your own becoming.

How do you feel?

____

____

____

____

____

____

____

____

____

____

Personal Hell

Drowning in the abyss that is this living hell,
regret is a constant whisper in my ear. But
beyond the smoke, a small breath flickers–
soft as a flame in a rain-worn room.

The ash may cling to my lungs, yet a
stubborn light persists–barely, like a candle
tucked in a cracked window. Hands reach,
not to pull me under, but to test the air, to
offer a name, to anchor me to a shore I
cannot yet see.

Love lingers in quiet corners: a warm mug
warming cold hands, a note tucked in a
pocket, a call that never quite ends. Trust
can be rebuilt, even if fragile as moth wings,
even if the day seems swept with fog.

I lie on the cold stone of memory, but the
rocks are not the whole floor. A door stands
nearby, rusted but patient, whispering of
hinges, of possibility if I choose to lift the
latch. Past, present, and a sliver of future
mingle in the breath I borrow.

This isn't home yet, not by a long shot, but the ruin holds a seed: a path that winds toward light—through rain, through doubt, through fatigue. Needs may go unanswered for a while, and love may sting, but there are mornings when the sky thins its gray and shows a pale blue.

When eyelids fall, they are not final; they are a pause, a seat by the window. In that quiet moment, I listen for a mild, stubborn hope: that maybe, the next breath is lighter, that I can stand, then walk, toward a day worth naming.

How do you feel?

____

____

____

____

____

____

____

____

____

____

____

____

Missing Pieces

Emotion surrounds us like the light of the moon, soft silver pooling in the corners of the room. How we talk is how we feel– words lifting like a tide, carrying the salt of our moods across air-chilled skin. How we move is what we want to shake off and leave behind, a shadowy wisp of dust trailing our steps as we go.

You miss it once it's gone– that pale halo, the quiet hum of presence– and the room remembers your voice even when you've left it like a doorway left open, breath fogging the frame. Picture the moment: a lamp sighs, thin rain tapping the window, and the floor gathers traces of footprints and emotion, every step rinsed by memory.

How do you feel?

____

____

____

____

____

____

Cold

A flower rots in winter, a bloom betrayed by frost, a feeling seeded inside the body, hushing the breath. Death wears this cold at the edges—purple with frost's kiss, fingers stiff as icicles, hair shedding like brittle snow. My blood is not ice; it remembers warmth, a distant heat that hums. Frozen within this vast cold, a quiet cathedral of ice.

And yet, I am still alive.

I carry the ache as a lantern in a dark room, not to banish night, but to name what remains. Iron-tasted air; rain-stung skin; the memory of heat lingering in the bones. Somewhere inside, a stubborn pulse keeps time with the world. The world outside may be white and merciless, but a small ember stays: I am here. I endure. I endure the thaw.

How do you feel?

Me—Others

Living—breathing—thinking—me; caring—
listening—nurturing—others.

How do you feel?

____

____

____

____

____

____

____

____

____

____

____

____

____

____

____

____

____

____

____

____

____

Heartless

Your voice is my beacon of hope; your name breathes life into me. Living without a path is like living without a heart –unmoved by anything, walking in a lifeless drift. You awaken the call to care for others, as I should have lived this truth from the start.

How do you feel?

____

____

____

____

____

____

____

____

____

____

____

____

____

____

____

____

____

Selfish

Seeing the souls on this earth, all confused about what they know, don't be misguided by all the knowledge of this material plane, for what you envision becomes a manifestation of reality. Be selfish in the path you choose, regardless of others' judgmental gaze. Being selfish becomes a quality of its own, free from the prying eyes of frugal hearts. If you don't have faith in yourself, simply ask, How can I be...me?

How do you feel?

____

____

____

____

____

____

____

____

____

____

____

____

Out

Streams moving, emotions ever turning, coming out of the dark, yet hiding in the light.

How do you feel?

Manifest

Embrace the life you live, envision the life you desire, and rise beyond the pain that once held you back.

How do you feel?

____

____

____

____

____

____

____

____

____

____

____

____

____

____

____

____

____

____

____

____

Silent Pain

I bear the pain in secrecy, saying nothing while others pretend not to see. When the truth leaks out, they vanish; if anyone asks what I have to say, I answer with silence.

How do you feel?

____

____

____

____

____

____

____

____

____

____

____

____

____

____

____

____

____

____

____

Confusion

Do they really love me, or is it all a lie, an illusion I mistake for truth? As my loneliness deepens, I hear no voice calling out—why? Is this a dream without end, my mind lost in the fog of what's happening? Do they...love me?

How do you feel?

____

____

____

____

____

____

____

____

____

____

____

____

____

____

____

____

____

____

Trickery

Hypnotized by thy gaze, deceiving the soul; trickery wounds more than knives. Watching yourself burn in your own flesh, you ignore the pain, while trickery's warm brush caresses you.

How do you feel?

____

____

____

____

____

____

____

____

____

____

____

____

____

____

____

____

____

____

Little by Little

Little by little, the heart beats in the ceaseless stream, refusing to flee the message that calls. Days unroll within, none can hide, for you are never lost.

How do you feel?

____

____

____

____

____

____

____

____

____

____

____

____

____

____

____

____

____

____

____

Revealed by Light

Through the graveyard I walk, unsure of
where I head; tombstones rise like a march
of silent soldiers. Fear threads its memory
through my mind, ready to pull me under. A
black figure trails, I run, I hide, until a calm
voice breathes: don't let go—please. The
figure leads me toward light, and I wonder
who saves me from the dark. From shadow
to brightness, I glimpse the face—it's you.
You laugh, racing down the hill; I follow
where you go. We climb a tree beside the
water, your presence bright as you watch the
tide. We move on toward the river, land on
the ground, and your voice lessens my doubt,
each word making my heart bright. We drift
to a sunlit patio, your light warming me from
within. Could this be love? I rise to leave,
you pull me close, and for a moment we're
frozen. Then your voice—loving, clear—says,
I love you, and you fade as I step back
toward home, hoping to return again.

How do you feel?

Pain Turns to Love

Morning after morning, I study the reflection that feels as if I'm a walking superstition of bad luck within my own skin, wondering if anyone would notice my absence. A flood of thoughts rushed into my caving mind, tearing apart my already departed thoughts. Scripts of misery I can't rewrite. Darkness pools at every corner of the room; the sun becomes a pale rumor, the moon a chilling witness to the only light glistening in the void. Shifting through the photos of memories wanting to relive, reenvisioning a time where the earth halted and time stood still, weeping for a time when you and I seemed almost within reach, a time where the tip of our fingers touched before turning our backs towards different lives. A knock shatters the stillness within the room from the glass window. I rise, trembling at the unknown of what would be beyond the prison of my own making.

At a glance, opening the window formed a gateway to escape the voided subconscious long past to find light and a sudden, unfamiliar warmth. They smile with soft eyes and ask me to come with them on an escape to move forward, never looking back at the moonlit room, overwhelmed by the mercy swirling around me. I step into their perimeter, leaving the room behind. They carry no threat, only a quiet intention to help. It's as if they sensed my pain, a guardian angel in plain clothes. With them, a radiant spear of peace penetrates the ground beneath me, shattering the ground of meaningless thoughts and past memories no longer serving a purpose—their gentleness as we walk away from all the chains I have made throughout the years, the soft edge of unyielding hope. For the first time, my mind is clear, making room for future endeavors. How did I become lucky when, in the past, I was the superstitious one? The past dissolves, memories chipping away like footprints in the mud. They knew what I needed to become, giving up all ties of what once secluded me in the past, to become the person I needed to become. I'll never forget this moment. At times, having someone nearby will drag you out of the voided room and into a glistening light.

How do you feel?

My Hidden World

Alone in my own world, I dwell in the shadows as tears rain down, drowning in a lake that's long since dried. Clouds smother the sky; the sun is nowhere to be found. On my knees, I'm tethered to a road that goes nowhere. My heart, once open to love, is now sealed tight. Breath fogs the air; everything turns to frost, while my body yields to ice. Frozen, my fingers chip away; the sting of my flesh keeps me shivering yet numb from the exposure. The cruel truth remains: I'm still alive. Within a long, withering time passing, I began to thaw, the lake thick with frost and the crimson of my fingertips. I can't scream, only detached. Why should I go on if there's nothing in the world that gives meaning or purpose? I mend others' sorrows, help them rise, only to watch them leave, blind to the devastation I've written in my own heart. Anxiety gnaws at me, hyper-aware of others' emotions, swayed by what people say. No one truly knows how I feel. I sacrificed my life for them, and it became a mistake—a regret that should never have happened. I wanted to love, and I did, but you arrived and drained me dry, leaving me with nothing.

How do you feel?

____
____
____
____
____
____
____
____
____
____
____
____
____
____
____
____
____
____
____
____
____
____
____

Tearing Heart

Roses erupt in relentless growth, vines gripping the earth as if to pull me down and ground me. Thorns guard me from harm, while a pounding heartbeat resounds—unfindable, as I search the world for an answer. By the lake, a figure sits on a bench as the sun slides toward the horizon. Their eyes meet mine at first glance, hair rippling in the breeze, legs crossed, elbows on the bench, watching the sunset. I cry, drawn to the quiet compassion in their gaze, wondering why the roses surged so fast and why that pulse in my chest grew louder. It seems to lead me to you. I almost fear the moment I sit beside them, yet the tear-wet beauty of their presence overwhelms me; nothing could be more astonishing. I glimpse the one I finally want. Finding them wasn't easy, yet it wasn't as complicated as it might have seemed.

How do you feel?

Apart

Finding the perfect gift, only to have to take it back, my heart tears open, and I drop to my knees, wanting to walk away. But I can't. In giving, I've found joy, the ache, and the warmth of love repeating itself. Then you said no, and the spell breaks.

How do you feel?

____

Guilt

Guilt is nothing more than an emotion, that's what they say, but like every emotion, you can shake it off–this one you can't. An everlasting abyss, the darkest creatures circle you, fear shaking you loose from breath or sleep. Guilt keeps you awake at night, forcing you to replay that day again and again, a break that never comes. And the only cure to ease the pain is love.

How do you feel?

____

____

____

____

____

____

____

____

____

____

____

____

____

____

Night Light

The moon, a silent puppeteer, pulls at the strings of my already shattered heart. What more could this night demand of me? What pain have I not shouldered in this life? I've had enough–why must there be more on the horizon?

How do you feel?

____

____

____

____

____

____

____

____

____

____

____

____

____

____

____

____

____

My Light

Looking into their eyes, I discover a beauty I hadn't known before. The stars glare with envy at your glow, the moon wanes in the presence of your luminescence. A beacon carried with me, bright as day in every place ventured, and I, forever drawn, shall never go blind.

How do you feel?

____

____

____

____

____

____

____

____

____

____

____

____

____

____

____

____

Why?

We release each other's hands and drift down separate roads, and my heart unravels with ruthless ache. I think of you constantly— my heart seeks your love, my body seeks your warmth. The fear of surrendering everything haunts me, yet your presence could make me whole again. I would never abandon you, consumed by sorrow, and let sadness become an overwhelming burden. As the world speculates our love is only beginning to bloom, comes the moment of authenticity that non-believers never measured. I meet the one who holds the key, opening the veil between two hearts, vowing never to quit watching your light, never to retreat from your presence, even as a future day arrives when your light spills over the shadows.

How do you feel?

Mistake

Ever mindful of the risks you take, consider the mistakes you'd rather forget, for those missteps may guide the path ahead on your own journey. If you don't learn from them, nothing is accomplished; everyone bears slips they wish to rewrite. Courage lives in embracing those mistakes, turning them into fuel as time flows on. When truth finally surfaces from the heart, you'll feel the pull of blame and the hush of release, a balance of dark and light within you.

How do you feel?

____

____

____

____

____

____

____

____

____

____

____

____

Love and Light

The power of love brings the being, psyche, and soul into equilibrium. Devotion of oneself, fear dissolves, and doubt recedes, like a mist before the sun. Bow to nothing but your own merit, strong and centered both stem and stern, a beacon steady in the shifting, stubborn waters of the sea. Yearning may come in a kindred soul or somewhere beyond the material world, the firm belief you are always held in someone's hearth and home, a warm fire in the darkest night. Follow the path you're meant to walk, while a golden light surrounds your being, psyche, and soul. Guarding you from harm and guiding you toward dawn.

How do you feel?

____

____

____

____

____

____

____

____

Live and Learn

The past returns like a tide, dragging my worries and passions toward memories I've learned to face. Some memories I once despised become teachers, showing how they reshaped my being, for good or for ill. From what I've learned, I chart a path forward, preparing the ground for whatever future arrives.

How do you feel?

____

____

____

____

____

____

____

____

____

____

____

____

____

____

____

Not Alone

Hating the hour when darkness swallows me,
I ache—sick, wrung with pain, heavy with
guilt. Dead trees loom; shadows tuck
themselves away from my eyes. I walk
toward the moon, for that is all I can see
from a distance, stepping out of the gloomy
forest into an army of statues. Each pose
holds an emotion you might crave, a
mirrored echo of what you'd like to feel.
Down the dirt path, a shadow appears and
then dissolves into a path of voiding light, and
I pursue. I follow, tracing it into a realm of
memories that your heart must learn to glean
from what you've already known.

It is lost forever; it walks, and you follow,
until you reach the highest mountain. There,
what you see is no longer a shadow but your
spiritual guide. Behind you, the spirits who
travel with you—your steadfast chorus—
surround you, reminding you that you are
not alone in this world. The voices rise: we
will help you, we will guard and guide you.
Whenever you need us, just think of our
presence, and we will come. We love you.

Stepping from the moonlit night into a summer day, knowing you are not desolate beyond your future endeavors.

How do you feel?

Lost in Shadow

Surrounded by fog, running in every direction, trying to find a way out of the blinding trail, nothing in sight as if a voided desert enveloped the senses, suddenly, a gust of wind dispels the fog, and a glimpse of a figure appears before me. The figure moves as if time were no enemy. The ground beneath is looped in purgatory. I sprint to this unknowing figure –"Where did you go?" I whisper, eyes catching a ghost of movement to my left. A mighty tree anchors the scene, its bark wrinkled like weathered skin, its leaves sighing with a gloomy tremor. I move closer and glance up: the figure has climbed the branches, eyes lifted to the vast blue above. A breath of wind threads through the branches, and a whisper hums: "What if I were up there? Why am I not there?" Confusion coils inside me, and the whisper returns, more profound, mysterious: "Why am I not there? Why am I not happy? What did I do wrong?" They slide down the trunk of the tree, steel in their hands of resolve, and tilt their gaze toward the sky again, then to me. I step beside them, take their hand, and say, "You'll be okay. Have faith in yourself and the road you walk. You can be up there—trust that you can reach the top." Tears bead on their cheeks; I gather them against my chest, their head resting on my shoulder. "Everything will be okay. Everything will," I tell them, "For I see galaxies of possibility shining in you. It may not be what you expect, but that's what happens when you surprise yourself." I brush away the tears, tilt my mouth into a small smile, and feel the moment shift, as if a door to tomorrow has opened.

How do you feel?

____

____

____

____

____

____

____

____

____

____

____

____

Emotional Fog

Nothing is more certain than the doubt that gnaws when you feel smaller than your own thoughts. When it happens, everyone disappears, and you stand still, glaring at the moon above. What do you see but a hollow, a space where hopes and dreams cloud your mind? Then you draw your focus to the present, the moon's pale patience guiding you forward. The mood still lingers, yet a hush of possibility threads through the night. "Can you hear me–can you?" Tears stream down your face. You walk in sorrow toward a fog of black, a whisper hinting that there might be a brighter path beyond the next bend, and in your chest a small, stubborn courage begins to wake.

How do you feel?

____

____

____

____

____

____

____

Beautiful Rush

Reaching a high mountain, clouds hover above, and the sun carves a dim, unbearable beauty through them–the scene so stunning it feels like a fall you could not survive. Finding the one you seek is no easy road; it grows tiring as you gaze down at the people who love you. You turn your back to the cliff, memory after memory crowding in as you begin to tilt, with no turning back. In the moment you leave the top of the mountain, you plummet faster, and the sky itself becomes a silent, terrible beauty, every element snapping into place. You close your eyes, ready to vanish. But then time seems to pause, you float, and when you open them again, you glimpse a blur of a face, arms reaching–tenderly catching you. Tears spill down their cheeks, and you weep with them. If you fall with your back turned, you wonder who will see you, or if you must fall. Yet no matter how much pain you store within, how heavy the regrets you wish to forget, love remains a radiant ember, and with your tears it begins to shine, vanquishing the night.

How do you feel?

Out of the Dark

Thinking of you steadies me; whispering your name, soft as a sigh, and it travels through my veins. I stand on a cliff above the restless sea, sunset spilling diamonds across the water. The beauty halos my gaze, and I wonder how much hope I hold, how much faith I can endure. Whispers ride the breeze, calling my name; I turn, met by a forest of pure grief. Darkness clings to this dreadful place, lifeless, as creatures stare—yet I cannot see them. I walk through the dreadful forest, my name whispered in the air, a refrain that never quite dies down. Beyond the trees, the path begins to change: life reemerges, creatures of secrecy revealing themselves as beauty incarnate. The whisper of my name lingers, guiding me to a valley where the clouds part, pain loosens its grip, and the sun shines down. A sense of secrecy loosens into revelation as light takes hold and begins to glow.

How do you feel?

Locked

Before their gaze, I've never seen such a mystery: secrets pressed tight, begging to be freed. Chains weigh the heart from within, yet a key lies lost in the map of their memories.

How do you feel?

____

____

____

____

____

____

____

____

____

____

____

____

____

____

____

____

____

____

Stuck

Crashing tides coil around my body, and I cling to a rock as it drags me toward the heart of the sea. There is no life in sight, only a vast solitude that gnaws at my chest. My heart feels like dust; my body grows cold as chaos swirls above and below. I ache for the halt of time, for a chance to go back, but that past is gone—too late to return. My choices have hardened into chains within me, and I cast the key into the ocean's unyielding tide. As that sea starts to settle, rain threads down my face, and in the ache of tears, I glimpse premonitions of the memories that once occurred: I have wept for this day. Though the current seems strong, a small ember of resolve kindles within me, choosing to say lit with nothing but faith and the grave of ash beneath, to seek a gentler shore, to trust a new day can begin beyond the horizon.

How do you feel?

Truth

Coming into oneself, facing truth, fighting for love, trying to keep one's sanity.

How do you feel?

Hopes and Dreams

Lost in an unforgettable maze, the walls feel familiar as I turn to pure nothingness. The maze reshapes into trees, circling me in a wooden crown that shades the sun. A pool glimmers at my side, and I watch others wander this world, their hopes and dreams unread, perhaps ungranted, swimming within those waters. I sit on the rocks, surrounded by silence, my hopes crushing into dust as thoughts of what wounds me press in. Yet even as I long for what brings me love, the water's reflection reminds me that change remains possible: each person contemplates what they wish to alter, and I wonder—will they ever reach that wish?

How do you feel?

Frozen

Coming out from the blankets, I sit up and greet the sunrise. I turn and find an envelope at the side of my bed, addressed to only I – "goodbye" is what it meant; "leaving" is what they did. I turn back toward the sun as the wind rises, the building groans and begins to tilt toward night, and the moon shines down while rain fills the gaps between the walls.

How do you feel?

____

____

____

____

____

____

____

____

____

____

____

____

____

____

____

Hidden words

My flesh cracks like a parched desert floor, each tear a crust that fractures the skin. I cannot move away from the drumbeat of anguish; I only endure, listening as my heart keeps time with the ache. Dark clouds brood overhead, and my blood pools, the body thinning to a fragile white, yet the heartbeat remains a stubborn drum–strong, defiant. When I'm gone, when my body drifts from this earth, the heart will still drum on, while the words I've buried rise as ghosts. They ache to break their confinement, painful to keep within, tugging at the corners of my mouth and pressing the floodgates of feeling to the surface, a whisper that hones to you, telling you how I feel.

How do you feel?

____

____

____

____

____

____

____

I Hear You

I found your heart, I spot your lies, I feel your pain, I hear your cries. I see the mask you wear, and know you've carried more than you should. Don't tell yourself you're weak—I hear you; I listen to you, again and again.

How do you feel?

____

____

____

____

____

____

____

____

____

____

____

____

____

____

____

____

____

Home

My heart flutters with emotion; I feel at
home, warmth blooming in your embrace.
With this song in my ears, I sense love–
you're my home, the place where I belong.

How do you feel?

____

Tension

Tension claws at the skin, a thirst to shed this body and slip into tomorrow. My heart won't slow; I must stay steady, crossing over the edge of now. It's harder than they think–the mind won't sleep, dragging me toward the next day, toward a future that keeps slipping away as I reach for it.

Heat rises in my chest, a quiet furnace that makes me sweat with the ache of what's to come. I chase relief in ashes, the cigarette's pale flame a brief, hollow mercy. Drinking promises numbness, but the numbness never stays. What will? A question that won't quit, echoing through bone and breath.

Each dawn, I rise from the past, as if time itself were a bed I'm forced to leave. I face the present–only to turn and glimpse tomorrow's shadow, still unresolved. I'm tethered to worry like a string you can't cut, pulled toward the horizon I can't reach, and still I wake, again and again, weary of the future's quiet, relentless pull.

How do you feel?

My Shining Star

Waiting on the shore, gazing at the pond-quiet ocean under a generous full moon, the night feels right for this one person. With every footprint they left on the sandy shore, luminescence would follow, praising the angelic being before me. This moment flutters back the rhythm of the beating heart, as if doubt loosened its grip and scattered into the ocean. They sat beside me, a soft glow in their eyes, bouncing off the moonlight, and the world seemed to breathe with us. The water whispered in calm, the shore keeping our secrets. The moonlit tide framed us, to let this moment hold a piece of this undying scenery. We stood to move with the night, steps light, until resting on the shores' lustre.

How do you feel?

Questions:

1. **How did the use of AI-assisted editing specifically influence or shape the poetry and its editing?**

The incorporation of AI into my creative process significantly expanded my artistic boundaries. Struggling to find the right words to transform my thoughts into vivid, movie-like scenes, or in ways I can see it to make sense to someone reading my poetry, I turned to AI for assistance with editing. This technology was the push I needed, helping me articulate my vision more clearly. While I chose the layout and structure, I ensured that my authentic voice permeated the writing. Without AI, the book I envisioned would have remained unrealized, trapped in my mind, and the drafted pages would have long been forgotten. It provided the encouragement and direction I needed to make this book possible.

2. **Are there suggestions for how to use the blank sections most meaningfully?**

I encourage you to approach the blank sections with openness and creativity. Let your imagination flow freely. Draw, write, or engage in any form of expression that resonates with you. Do not confine yourself; these pages are a canvas for exploration and self-discovery. Use them as a space to unpack your thoughts, express your emotions, and engage deeply with yourself.

3. **What should a reader do if the poem brings up overwhelming emotions?**

If you feel overwhelmed while engaging with this book, I urge you to take a step back. Allow yourself the time to breathe and process your feelings. When you feel ready, revisit the book at your own pace. If any trauma surfaces, I highly recommend reaching out to the crisis hotline included in the book, confiding in trusted friends, family members, and/or therapists. Your safety and well-being are the utmost priority, so please take care of yourself.

4. **Is this book intended for those new to poetry, or for experienced poetry readers as well?**

This book is designed for everyone—whether you are a newcomer to poetry, have some experience, or are well-versed in the art form. My intention is to inspire and support all readers, regardless of their background. The poems are crafted to provide a meaningful experience that fosters personal growth and reflection.

5. **What personal healing or transformation did the author experience through writing this book?**

The journey of writing this book was profoundly transformative, though not without its challenges. I realized that the chaotic words swirling in my mind were my subconscious urging me to seek help. My self-confidence was fragile, and I often found myself grappling with vast emotions. I sought guidance from a therapist as I navigated these feelings, particularly during my darkest moments when I struggled to see the light at the end of the tunnel. This exploration taught me that emotions are temporary, and it is how we respond to them that shapes our experience. I learned to acknowledge my worries without letting them consume me, and I discovered the importance of letting go of emotions beyond my control. This process took time, and while letting go is not a quick step, it is a vital part of living fully. I strive to practice this in my daily life, and I hope to share these insights through the poetics I bestow upon you.

A question someone asked me

I had someone ask me why I act funny sometimes and why I don't always act my age. I answered, as if I were an elder, with a question: If you were on your deathbed, would you have regrets? When the other person labeled the conversation as dark, I replied, "If you think this is dark, you're not really contemplating what life means." Time doesn't pause for anyone, and too often we chase the clock instead of living.

Many of us, including myself, believed that when you're young, you're immortal and can do anything you set your mind to. Everyone has strengths and weaknesses. Some people would rather stay in bed and avoid reality. It feels as if we forget–and I forget too–that when we know we can do anything, the motivation is not there because we imagine time stacked away. When we're older and slower, we suddenly want to do something as if we have the endurance to finish it. We tell ourselves we'll get it done, but often that day, month, or year never arrives.

Seventeen years can pass while we're writing about something we could have started long ago (obviously, I'm talking about myself). We may live one day and be gone the next–we don't know when our time will run out or how fast it will go.

Meditation and visualization exercise

Here is a technique you could try if you ever feel like no one misses you, that no one will miss you when you're gone, that everyone will forget you even existed, or that you mean little in the world. I want to tell you that at least one person in this world—and more—wants you to keep on living. I know this may not mean much when you're in a state of emptiness, and it can be hard to accept a compliment or to remember what caring or love truly feels like. If you have thoughts of self-harm or you have a plan, I urge you to seek help. Your life is worth living.

I want to share a visualization exercise I find powerful. Don't let that word fool you—the technique helped me when I was mentally exhausted and felt like the hollow shell of my heart, unsure whether I cared about anything or whether anyone would miss me. Emotions may come up during this exercise, and you might feel uncomfortable. If you don't feel ready, that's absolutely okay—there's no pressure. If you complete it, you may experience a shift in mindset, though outcomes vary from person to person.

You're welcome to play calming or mood-appropriate music as you proceed. The technique is called "open casket." In this exercise, you visualize your own funeral taking place. This may feel dark or uncomfortable, but the contrast between the visualization and real life can illuminate what truly matters. There can be a bright ending to this, even if it feels difficult at first.

Important note: If you'd like to read ahead, I recommend doing so. This exercise is not meant to trigger anyone; my aim is to remind you that every life is precious. If you're experiencing mental distress or thoughts of self-harm, please talk to someone you trust and seek professional help. If you need immediate support, crisis resources are available. You are not bothering anyone by reaching out, and those who dismiss your need aren't the right people to help you.

Open Casket

1. Sit in a comfortable position with your eyes closed. Begin with a slow inhale, followed by a slow exhale, releasing the pressures of daily life.

2. As you breathe, count down from 10 to 1. For example: inhale and exhale 10, then 9... 8... 7... 6... 5... 4... 3... 2... and 1. It's okay if your mind isn't tranquil yet; with practice, visualization, and meditation, it will help calm over time.

3. When you're ready, lie on your back and cross your arms on your chest, or lay your arms close to your sides. Stay calm during this process.

4. Imagine your body lying inside a casket, in a building of your choosing. Feel the white silk from the pillow and sheets. Is there a smell? What are you wearing? Do you hear crying or voices? Is there music playing? What color is your skin? Who do you think is talking at your funeral? Use all of your senses.

5. Now visualize your friends and family coming to your open casket, one by one, talking to you and choking on their words, shedding tears, wishing this wasn't the outcome. Each person comes by to say goodbye. Spend some time hearing what they have to say.

6. Keep envisioning yourself still within the coffin, but now in the cemetery with your loved ones gathered around you. Step out of the coffin and look at the tombstone before you–your name, birth, and death. Consider what they put on your stone. You try to speak to the family as the priest reads from the script. No matter how many tears they shed, nothing will bring you back; no matter how loudly you scream, you won't be heard. Then you see it: your body within the casket, lifeless. Suddenly, you are jolted back in the casket. You hear the priest closing the lid and locking the opening. You hear faint mumbles.

7. As the coffin is slowly lowered into the earth, feel your body sinking with it. Hear the dirt covering your casket. You are now frozen in time. Do you think time is stopping? Do you notice your mistakes, the cries of others, knowing you can't go forth and breathe again? What emotions are you feeling? Let them out.

8. Now, while you are still in the ground, envision life returning to your body as a radiant light. Sit up into a seated position and imagine breaking from the confines of the casket, crawling out of the dirt, and standing on the soft grass beneath. Look at the sky–the bright sky, the green grass, the clean, crisp air. Soak in everything you see.

9. Walk out of the cemetery and become alive to this new beginning. People can see you; you are back in your physical form. Surround yourself with your friends, family, and everyone who cares about you. Remember: life is precious, and we cannot do this alone. You are important. Don't let anyone tell you that you are not enough. Be limitless. Be you.

How did you feel doing this visualization exercise? Did you cry? Was there happiness at the end? Who came to your funeral (don't say no one; I know people care about you).

Crisis Support Resources

If you or someone you know is experiencing emotional distress, feeling overwhelmed, or contemplating suicide, it's essential to reach out for help. You are not alone, and trained professionals are available to support you.

National Suicide Prevention Lifeline

Call: 988

The National Suicide Prevention Lifeline is a free, confidential service that is available 24/7. When you call, you will be connected to a trained counselor who can provide support, listen to your concerns, and help you find resources in your area. The service is designed to assist individuals in crisis and those who are worried about someone else.

Crisis Text Line

Text: "HELLO" to 741741

For those who may feel more comfortable communicating via text, the Crisis Text Line offers a similar service. By texting "HELLO" to 741741, you'll connect with a trained crisis counselor who can provide immediate support and guidance. This option is available 24/7 as well.

Why Reach Out?

Reaching out for help is a sign of strength. Whether you're feeling hopeless, anxious, or just need someone to talk to, these resources are there to listen without judgment and to help you explore options for moving forward.

Remember: It's okay to ask for help. Your mental health matters, and people care and want to help you through difficult times.

References

"Unraveling the Meaning of the Suicide Prevention Ribbon: An Essential Guide to 988 and National Suicide Prevention Resources." *Brian Sharp Counseling*, www.briansharpcounseling.com/post/unraveling-the-meaning-of-the-suicide-prevention-ribbon-an-essential-guide-to-988-and-national-suic.
I accessed the website at 11.25.25.

www.ingramcontent.com/pod-product-compliance
Lightning Source LLC
LaVergne TN
LVHW090612110826
845146LV00001B/359

* 9 7 9 8 9 8 9 8 0 9 8 7 5 *